BRIGHT and EARLY BOOKS
for BEGINNING Beginners

This book belongs to …

_____

BEARS ARE CURIOUS

by Joyce Milton

illustrated by Christopher Santoro

Sandvik Publishing and associated logos are trademarks and/or registered trademarks
of Sandvik Publishing Interactive, Inc., Danbury, CT. SandvikPublishing.com

STEP INTO READING and colophon and BRIGHT AND EARLY BOOKS and colophon and
RANDOM HOUSE and colophon are registered trademarks of Penguin Random House LLC.

Printed in Melrose Park, Illinois, U.S.A.

Item #: 00001-844

SP20001160AUG2017

First Printing, November 2015

BEARS ARE CURIOUS

by Joyce Milton
illustrated by Christopher Santoro

A Bright and Early Book
From BEGINNER BOOKS®
A Division of Random House

Bears are curious.
They are almost always
hungry, too.

This mother bear
and her cubs
are looking
for food.

The mother bear
sniffs the air.
Her nose tells her
that bees are living
in the tree.

She sticks her paw
inside the tree.
Yum!
Sweet wild honey.

A few bees are stuck
in the honey.
The mother bear
eats them up!

The cubs lick honey
from her paw.
Angry bees buzz around.
The bears' thick fur
keeps them safe.

Why are the bears
so hungry?

All winter long,
the mother bear
stayed in a cave.
She did not eat
any food.

One winter day,
her cubs were born.
The cubs drank
their mother's milk.

Mother and cubs
cuddled to keep
warm.
They slept a lot.

Then spring came.
The mother bear was
thin and hungry.

She needed to find food
for herself
and her cubs.

A hungry bear will eat
lots of things.

Flowers.

Ants.
Beetles.

Acorns.

Berries.

Even mice!

It is summer.
The cubs follow
their mother.
She keeps them
safe.

An eagle
swoops down
at one of the cubs!
The mother bear
comes running.

The eagle flies away.

It is fall.
The mother bear
is fat again.
The cubs are fat, too.
They will spend
one more winter
together.

There are different
kinds of bears.
These are black bears.
Black bears are good
at climbing trees.

Brown bears are bigger
than black bears.
They have longer claws.

Some brown bears are
called grizzly bears.

Some bears catch fish.

This cub is learning.

He does a belly flop
on top of a fish.

Oops!
The fish got away.

Polar bears live
in the Arctic,
a land of ice and snow.
Their thick fur
keeps them warm.

Polar bears are
great swimmers.
They hunt seals
and walruses.

Young bears like
to explore.

Sometimes they wander
into towns.

One showed up at a
birthday party.
The cake was tasty!
But where were the guests?
They had all run away!

But bears *are* wild.
They can be dangerous.
This bear was lucky.
A ranger shot it
with a special dart.

The bear was not hurt.

He just fell asleep.

Rangers loaded him

into a truck.

When the bear woke up,
he was back in the woods.
Safe and sound.